The Vampire and the Lost Locket

by Kate Tremaine

illustrated by Jared Sams

Published in the United States of America by Cherry Lake Publishing Group
Ann Arbor, Michigan
www.cherrylakepublishing.com

Reading Adviser: Marla Conn, MS, Ed., Literacy specialist, Read-Ability, Inc.
Book Designer: Book Buddy Media
Photo Credits: page 1: ©djvstock / Getty Images; page 7: ©Hulton Archive / Getty Images; page 7:
©American / debatepolitics.com; page 7: ©MarjanNo / Pixabay (paper); page 7: ©Durova / Wikimedia;
page 11: ©vintagereveries102 / Flickr; page 11: © / goodfreephotos.com; page 21: ©VeraPetruk
/ Getty Images; page 25: ©Daria Ustiugova / Getty Images; page 25: ©johavel / shutterstock.
com; page 30: ©Shanina / Getty Images; page (background): ©ba888 / Getty Images

Torch Graphic Press is an imprint of Cherry Lake Publishing Group.

Library of Congress Cataloging-in-Publication Data
Names: Tremaine, Kate, author. | Sams, Jared, illustrator.
Title: The vampire and the lost locket / by Kate Tremaine ; illustrated by Jared Sams.
Description: Ann Arbor, Michigan : Torch Graphic Press, 2020. | Series: The Secret Society of Monster Hunters
    | Includes bibliographical references and index. | Audience: Ages 10-13. | Audience: Grades 4-6. | Summary:
    Fiona, Elena, and Marcus travel to Chicago in 1938 to help a vampire recover her stolen locket.
Identifiers: LCCN 2020016502 (print) | LCCN 2020016503 (ebook) | ISBN 9781534169395 (hardcover) |
    ISBN 9781534171077 (paperback) | ISBN 9781534172913 (pdf) | ISBN 9781534174757 (ebook)
Subjects: LCSH: Graphic novels. | CYAC: Graphic novels. | Vampires—Fiction. | Time travel—Fiction. | Secret
    societies—Fiction. | Depressions—1929—Fiction. | Chicago (Ill.)—History—20th century—Fiction.
Classification: LCC PZ7.7.T7 Vam 2020 (print) | LCC PZ7.7.T7 (ebook) | DDC 741.5/973—dc23
LC record available at https://lccn.loc.gov/2020016502
LC ebook record available at https://lccn.loc.gov/2020016503

Cherry Lake Publishing Group would like to acknowledge the work of the Partnership for 21st Century Learning,
a Network of Battelle for Kids. Please visit http://www.battelleforkids.org/networks/p21 for more information.

Printed in the United States of America
Corporate Graphics

TABLE OF CONTENTS

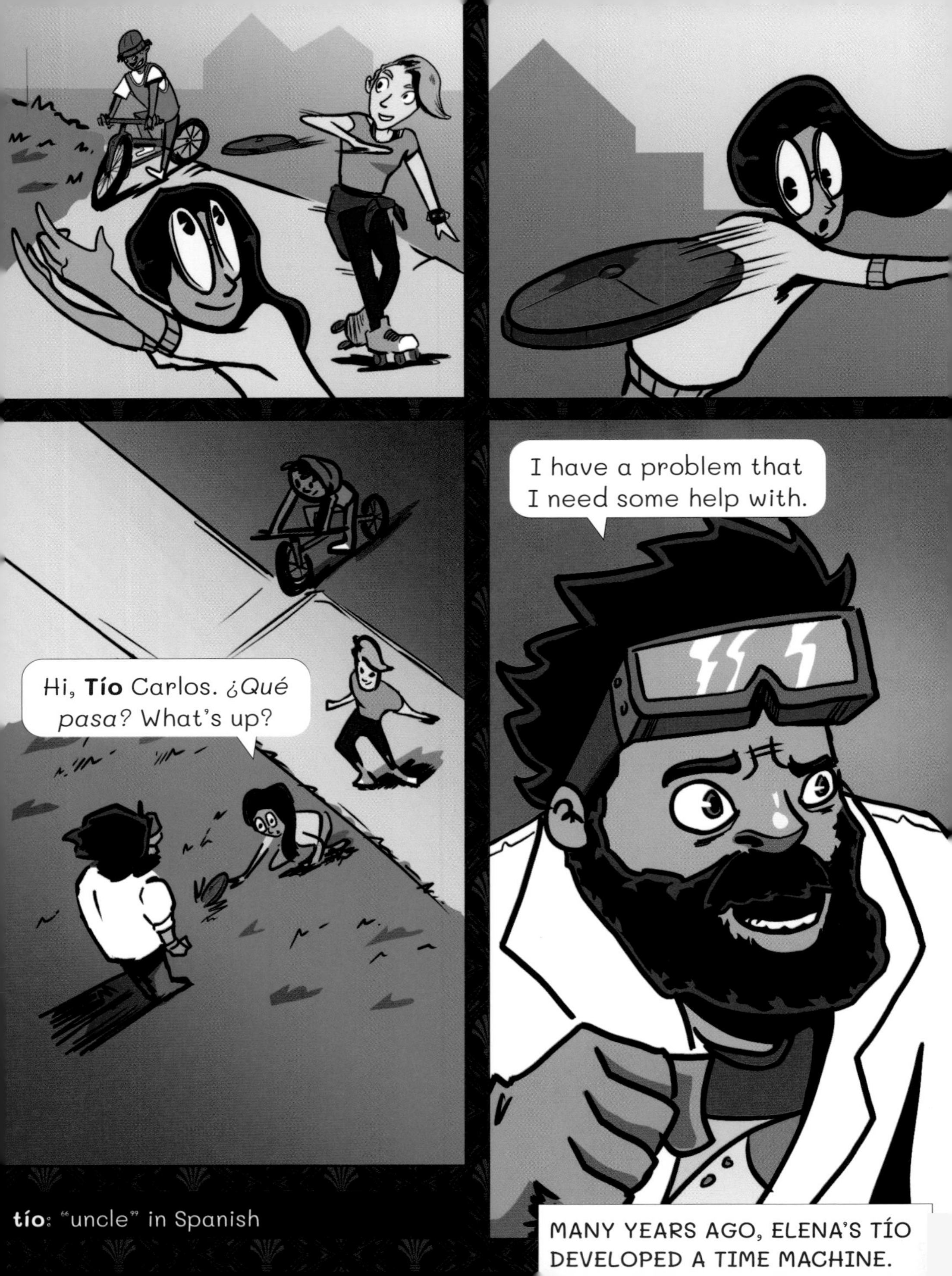
Hi, Tío Carlos. ¿Qué pasa? What's up?
I have a problem that I need some help with.
MANY YEARS AGO, ELENA'S TÍO DEVELOPED A TIME MACHINE.

tío: "uncle" in Spanish

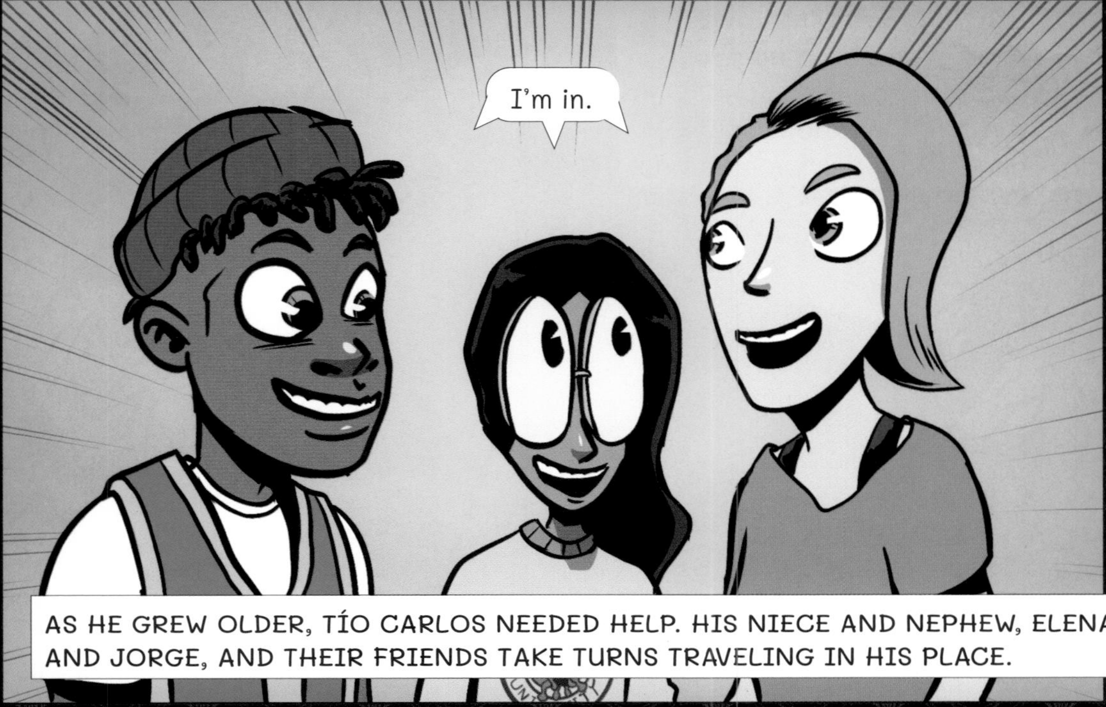
I'm in.
AS HE GREW OLDER, TÍO CARLOS NEEDED HELP. HIS NIECE AND NEPHEW, ELENA AND JORGE, AND THEIR FRIENDS TAKE TURNS TRAVELING IN HIS PLACE.

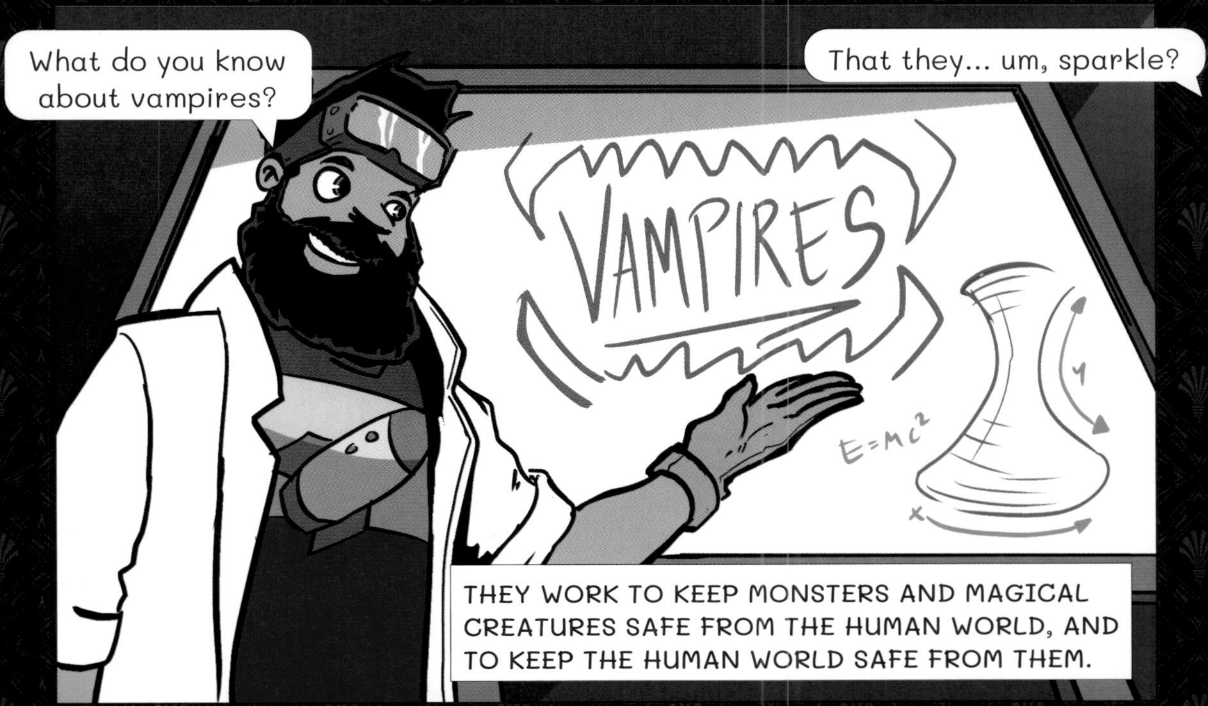
What do you know about vampires?
That they... um, sparkle?
VAMPIRES
E=MC2
THEY WORK TO KEEP MONSTERS AND MAGICAL CREATURES SAFE FROM THE HUMAN WORLD, AND TO KEEP THE HUMAN WORLD SAFE FROM THEM.

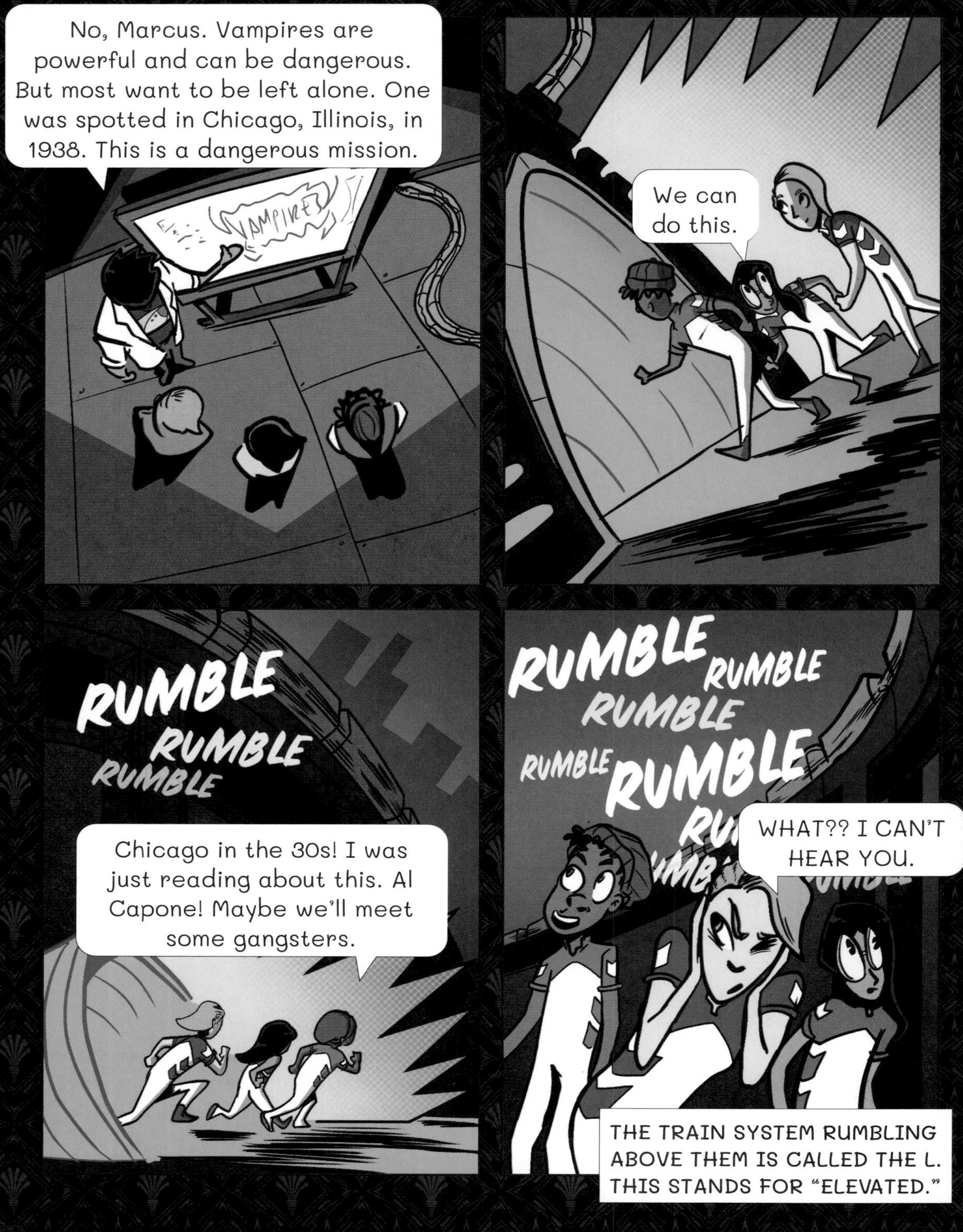
No, Marcus. Vampires are powerful and can be dangerous. But most want to be left alone. One was spotted in Chicago, Illinois, in 1938. This is a dangerous mission.
VAMPIRES
We can do this.
RUMBLE
RUMBLE
RUMBLE
Chicago in the 30s! I was just reading about this. Al Capone! Maybe we'll meet some gangsters.
RUMBLE RUMBLE
RUMBLE
RUMBLE RUMBLE
WHAT?? I CAN'T HEAR YOU.
THE TRAIN SYSTEM RUMBLING ABOVE THEM IS CALLED THE L. THIS STANDS FOR "ELEVATED."

TIPS FOR THE DECADE

The 1930s are known as the **Great Depression** because the economy was "depressed." Work was hard to find. Many cultural aspects of the 1930s were defined by the Great Depression.

* Soup kitchens fed people who couldn't buy food.

* The government, under President Franklin D. Roosevelt, created many programs to put people back to work. The programs were collectively called the New Deal.

By 1938, things had begun to improve. But then the economy had another **recession**.

* The "Dust Bowl" years of 1935 to 1938 were very hot and dry for the Midwest.

* Many farms failed. More than 2 million people headed to California or moved to Midwestern cities.

Great Depression: A great financial slump that began in 1929
recession: a period of time when the trade and business is not doing well

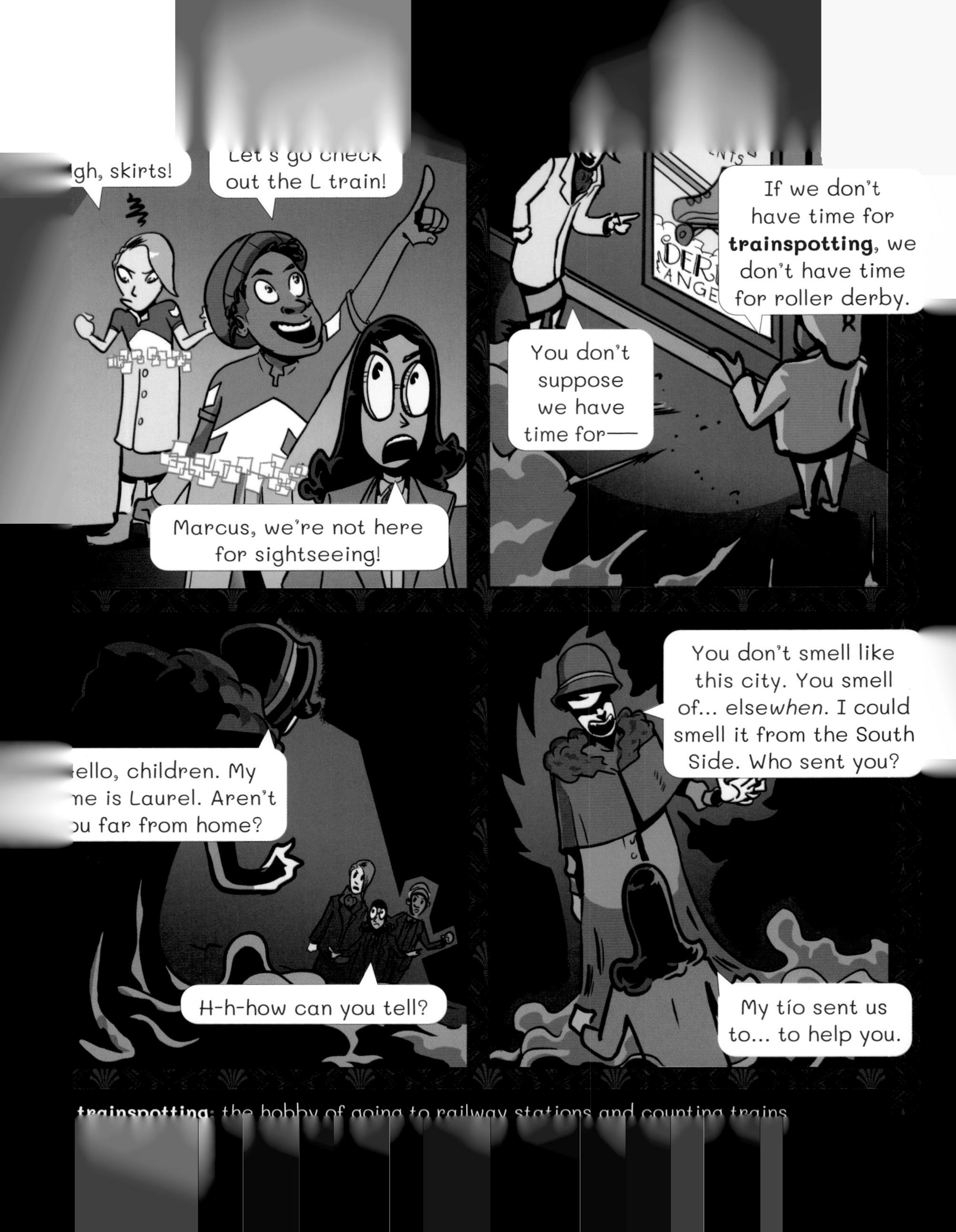
gh, skirts!
Let's go check out the L train!
Marcus, we're not here for sightseeing!
You don't suppose we have time for—
If we don't have time for **trainspotting**, we don't have time for roller derby.
ello, children. My me is Laurel. Aren't u far from home?
H-h-how can you tell?
You don't smell like this city. You smell of... else*when*. I could smell it from the South Side. Who sent you?
My tío sent us to... to help you.

trainspotting: the hobby of going to railway stations and counting trains

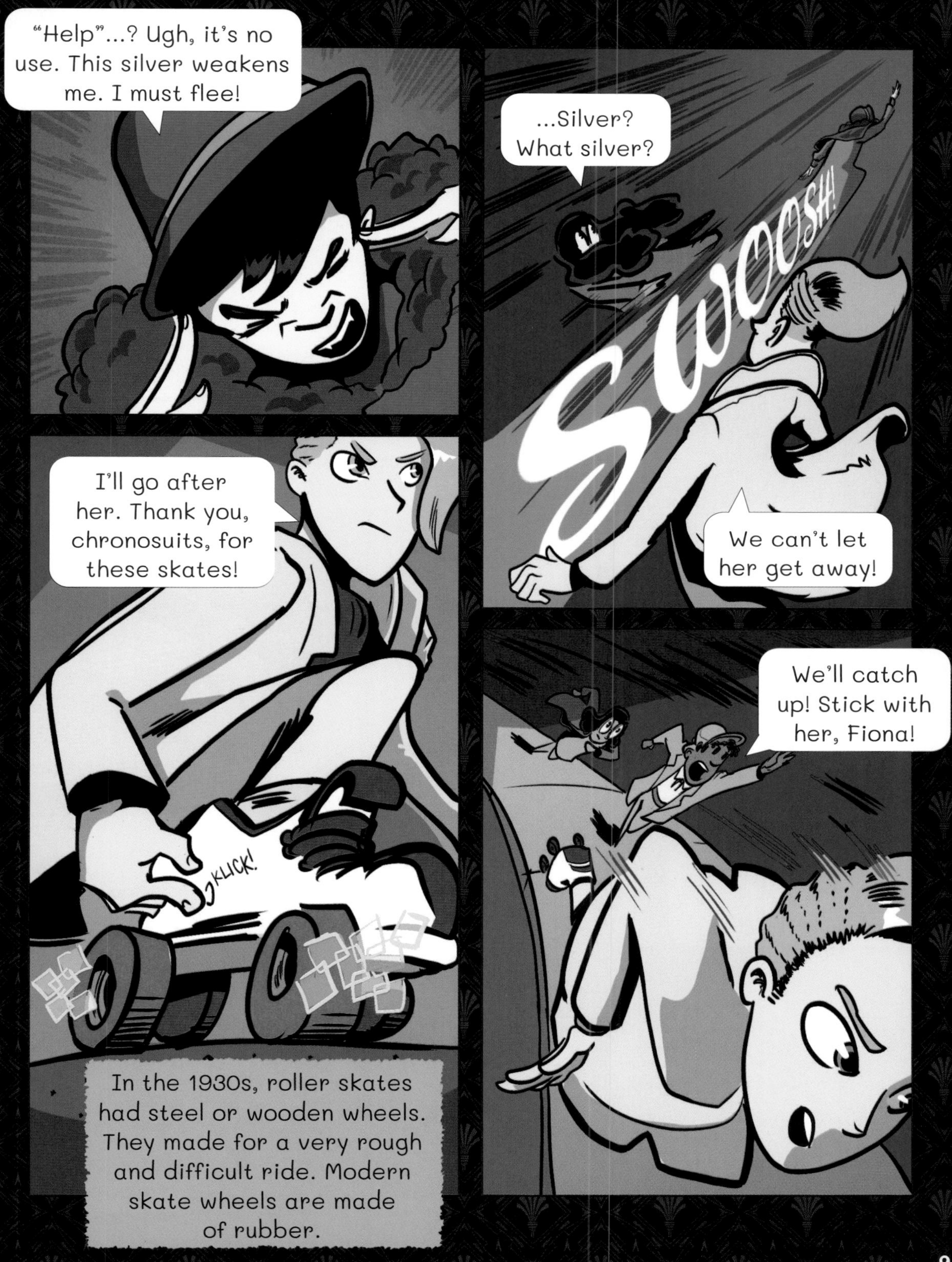
"Help"...? Ugh, it's no use. This silver weakens me. I must flee!
...Silver? What silver?
SWOOSH!
We can't let her get away!
I'll go after her. Thank you, chronosuits, for these skates!
KLICK!
In the 1930s, roller skates had steel or wooden wheels. They made for a very rough and difficult ride. Modern skate wheels are made of rubber.
We'll catch up! Stick with her, Fiona!

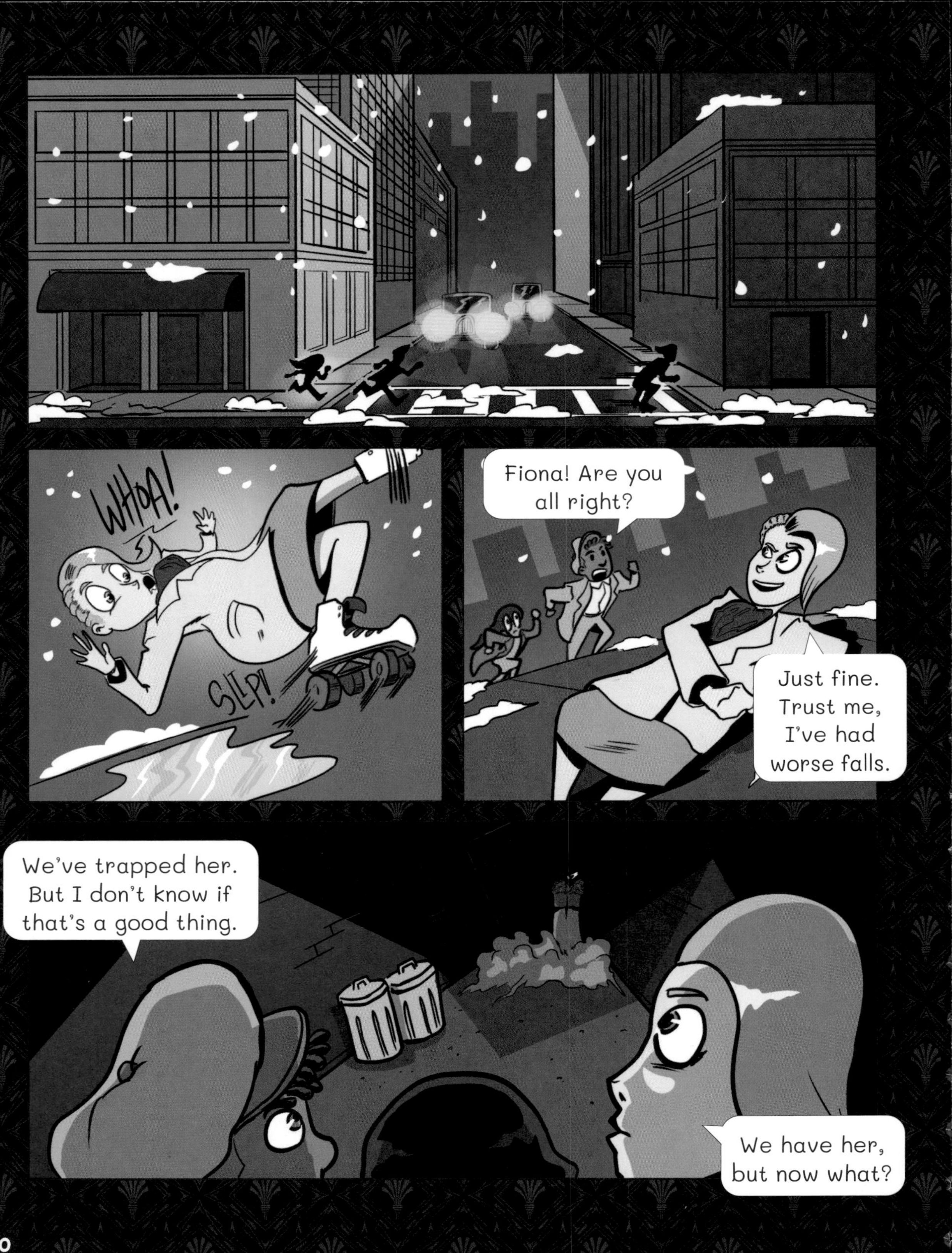
WHOA!
SLIP!
Fiona! Are you all right?
Just fine. Trust me, I've had worse falls.
We've trapped her. But I don't know if that's a good thing.
We have her, but now what?

PACKING LIST

* For women, simple dresses with bold prints
* For men, suits with shoulder pads and slim-cut arms
* Long coat with fur trim
* Accessories: newspaper, hats, overshoe roller skates

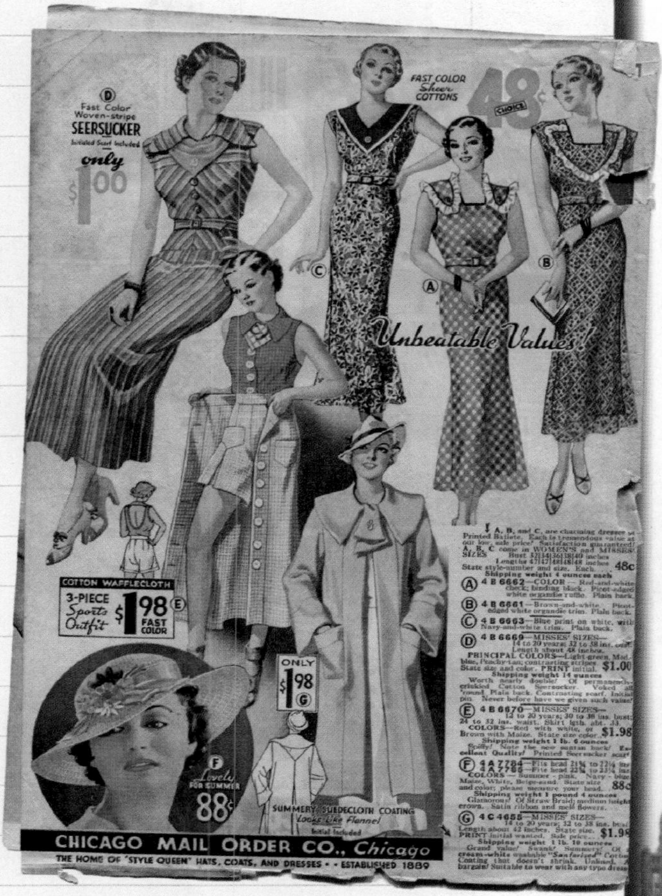
D
Fast Color Woven-stripe
SEERSUCKER
only
$1.00
FAST COLOR Sheer COTTONS
CHOICE
48¢
C
A
B
Unbeatable Values!
COTTON WAFFLECLOTH
3-PIECE Sports Outfit
$1.98
FAST COLOR
E
ONLY
$1.98
G
F
Lovely FOR SUMMER
88¢
SUMMERY SUEDECLOTH COATING
Looks Like Flannel
CHICAGO MAIL ORDER CO., Chicago
THE HOME OF "STYLE QUEEN" HATS, COATS, AND DRESSES • • ESTABLISHED 1889

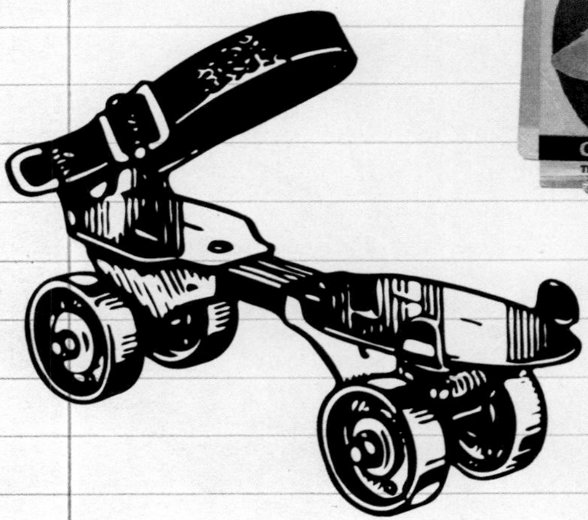

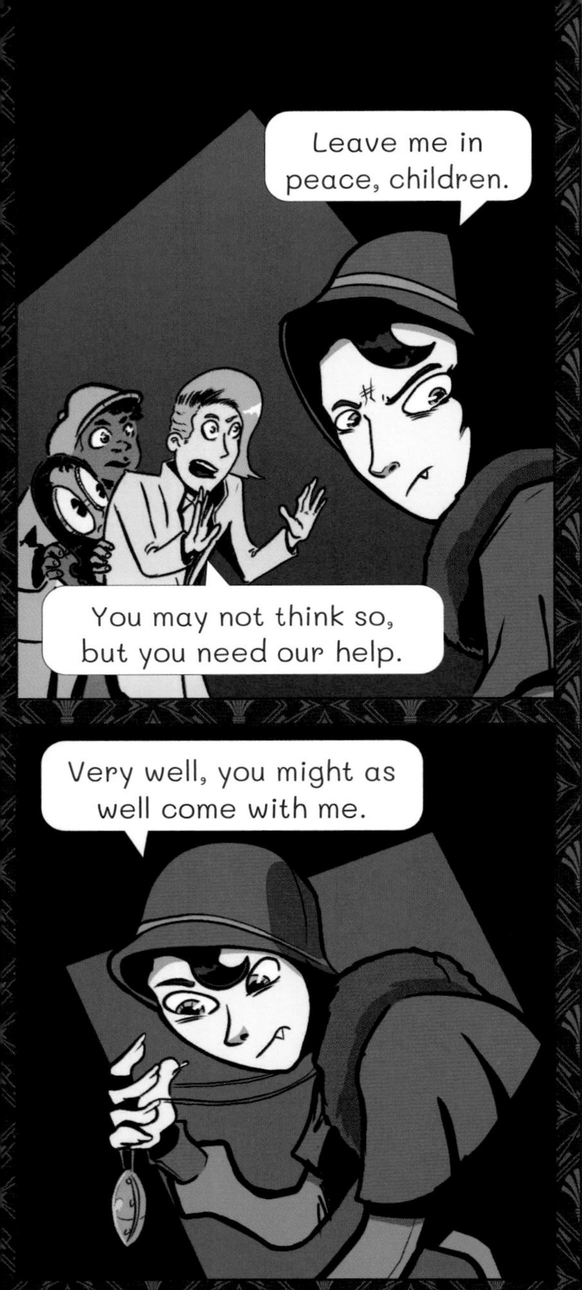
Leave me in peace, children.
You may not think so, but you need our help.
Very well, you might as well come with me.

locket: a small case, usually made of gold or silver, that is worn on a necklace chain

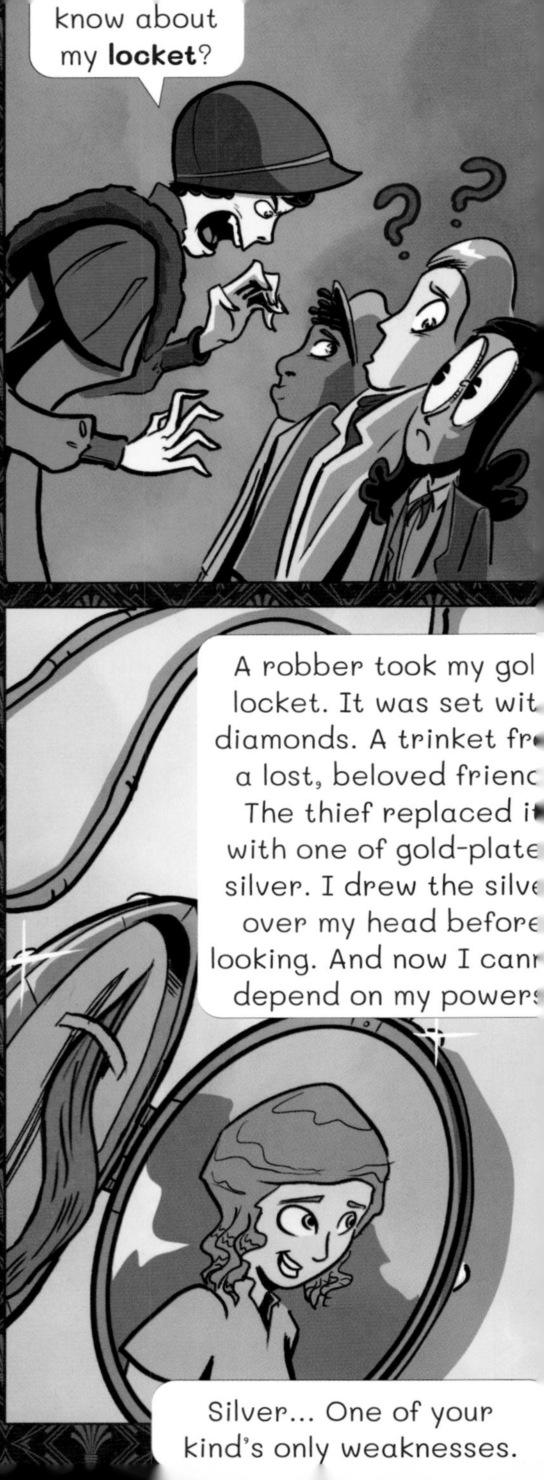
know about my **locket**?
A robber took my gol locket. It was set wit diamonds. A trinket fr a lost, beloved frienc The thief replaced it with one of gold-plate silver. I drew the silve over my head before looking. And now I canr depend on my powers
Silver... One of your kind's only weaknesses.

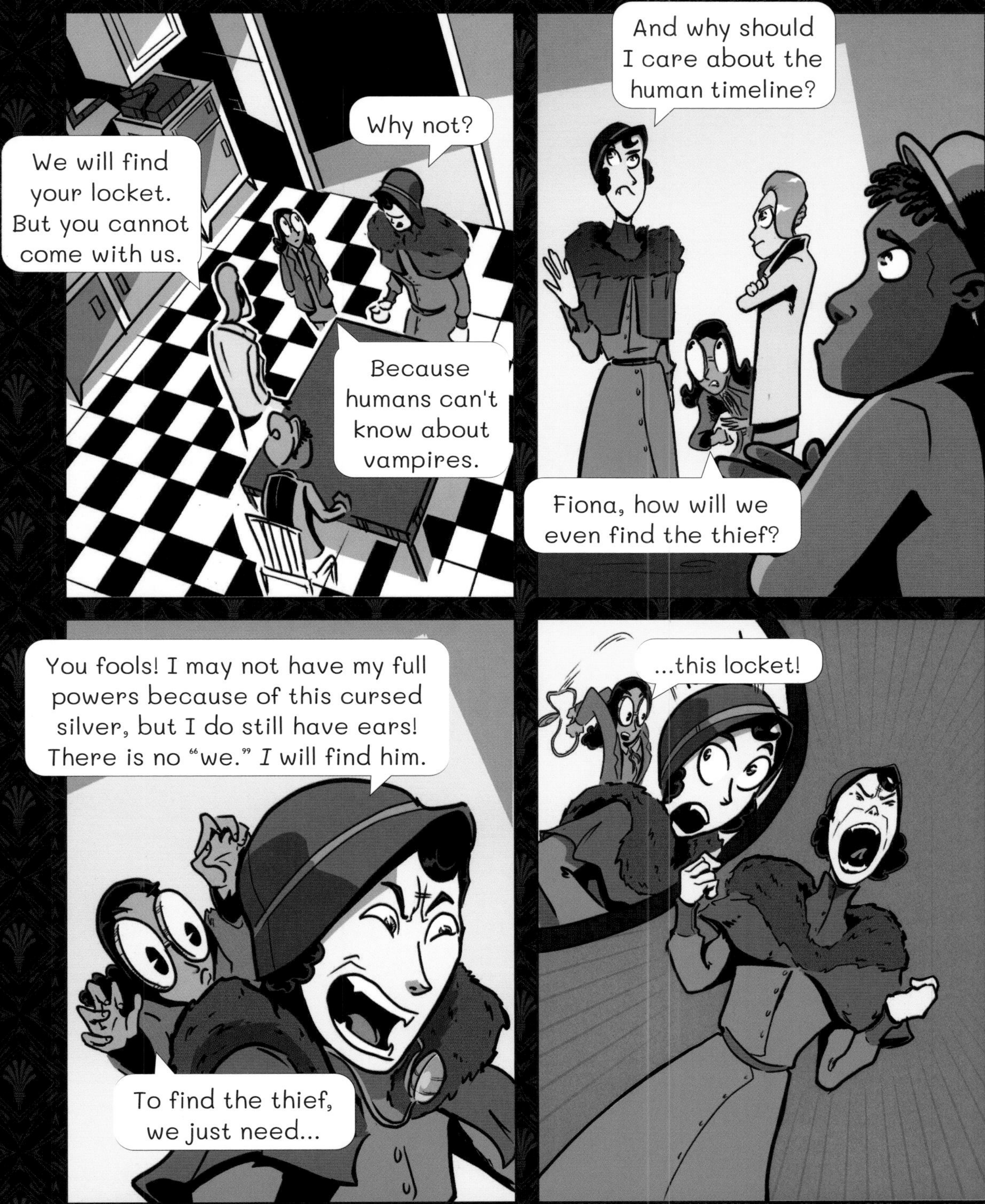
We will find your locket. But you cannot come with us.
Why not?
Because humans can't know about vampires.
And why should I care about the human timeline?
Fiona, how will we even find the thief?
You fools! I may not have my full powers because of this cursed silver, but I do still have ears! There is no "we." *I* will find him.
To find the thief, we just need...
...this locket!

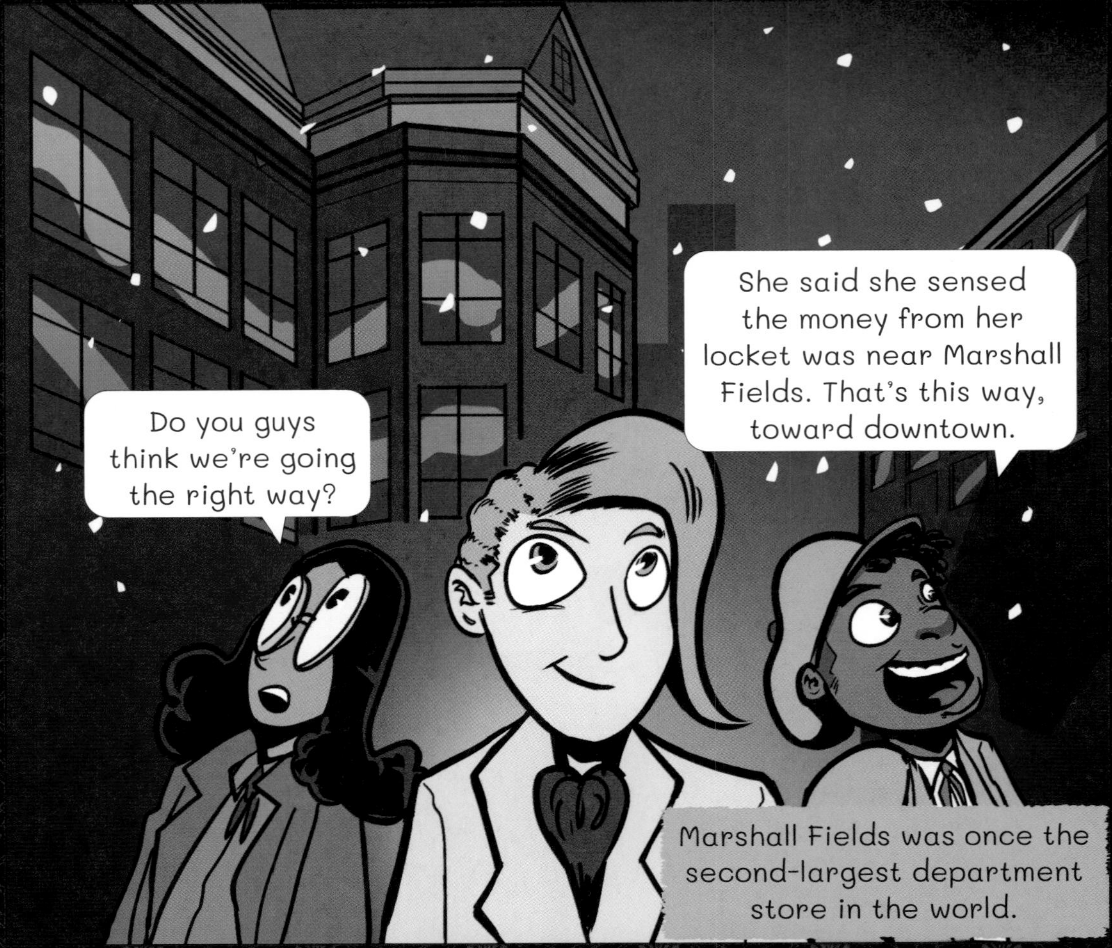
Do you guys think we're going the right way?
She said she sensed the money from her locket was near Marshall Fields. That's this way, toward downtown.
Marshall Fields was once the second-largest department store in the world.

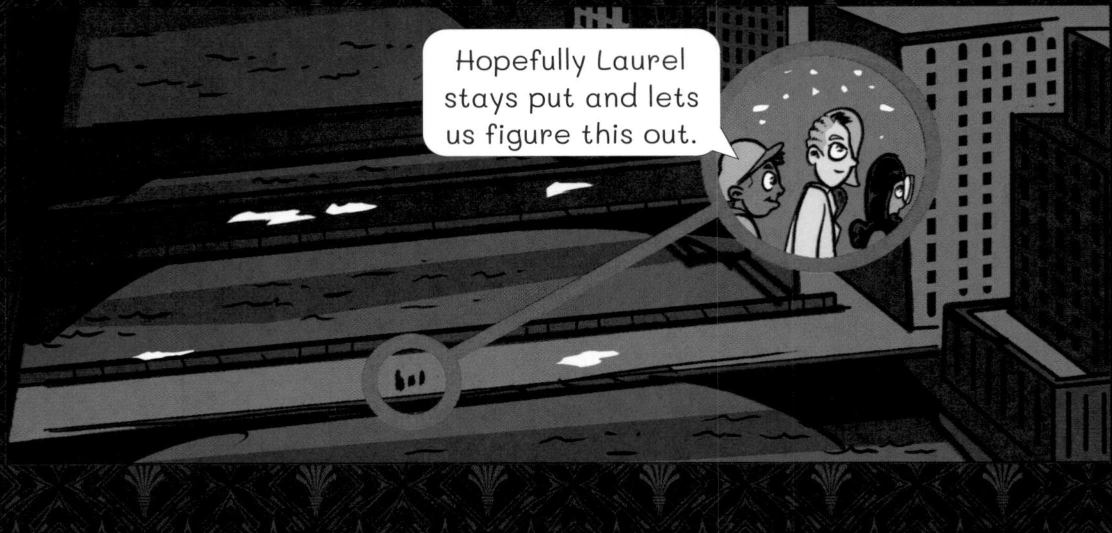
Hopefully Laurel stays put and lets us figure this out.

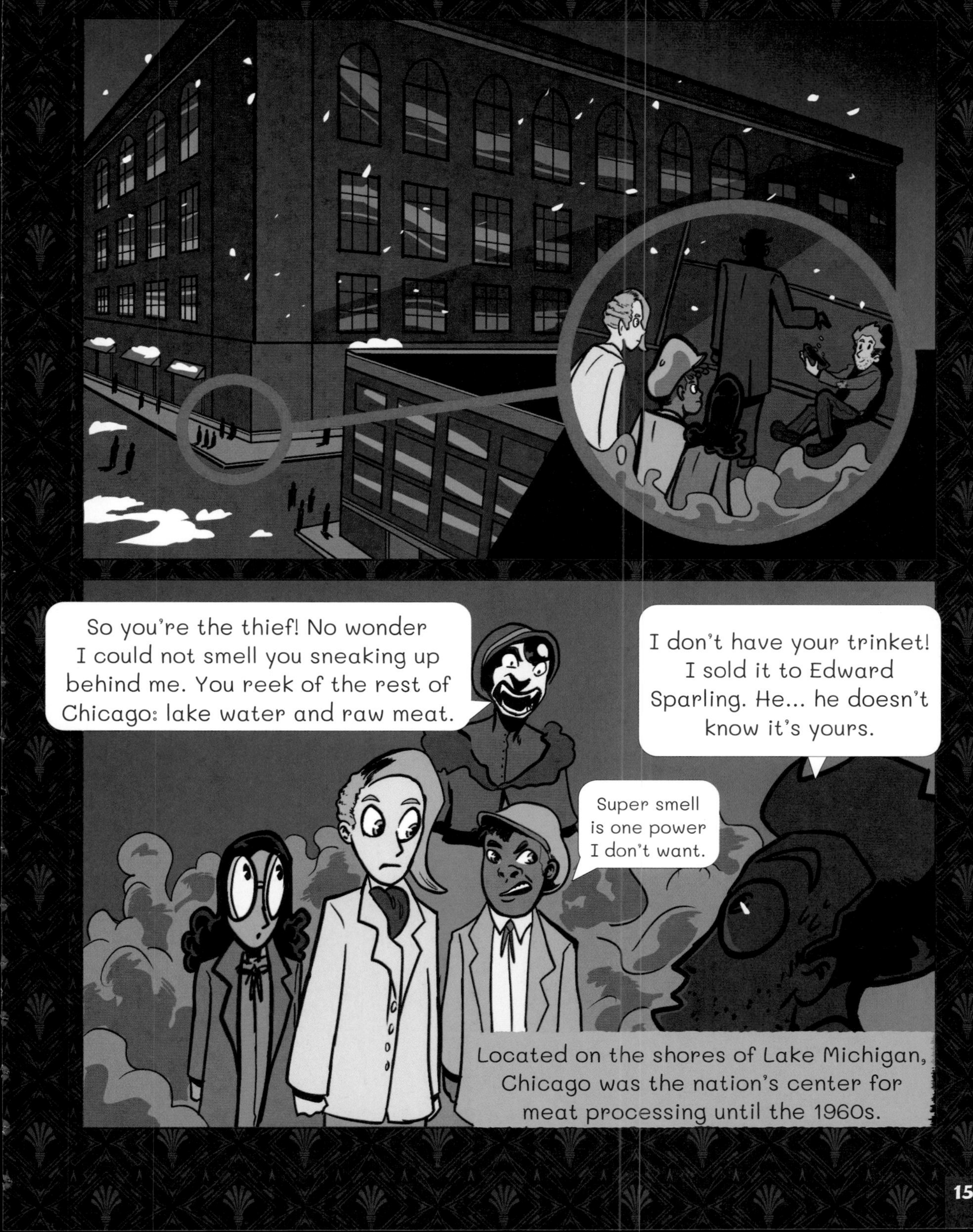
So you're the thief! No wonder I could not smell you sneaking up behind me. You reek of the rest of Chicago: lake water and raw meat.
I don't have your trinket! I sold it to Edward Sparling. He... he doesn't know it's yours.
Super smell is one power I don't want.
Located on the shores of Lake Michigan, Chicago was the nation's center for meat processing until the 1960s.

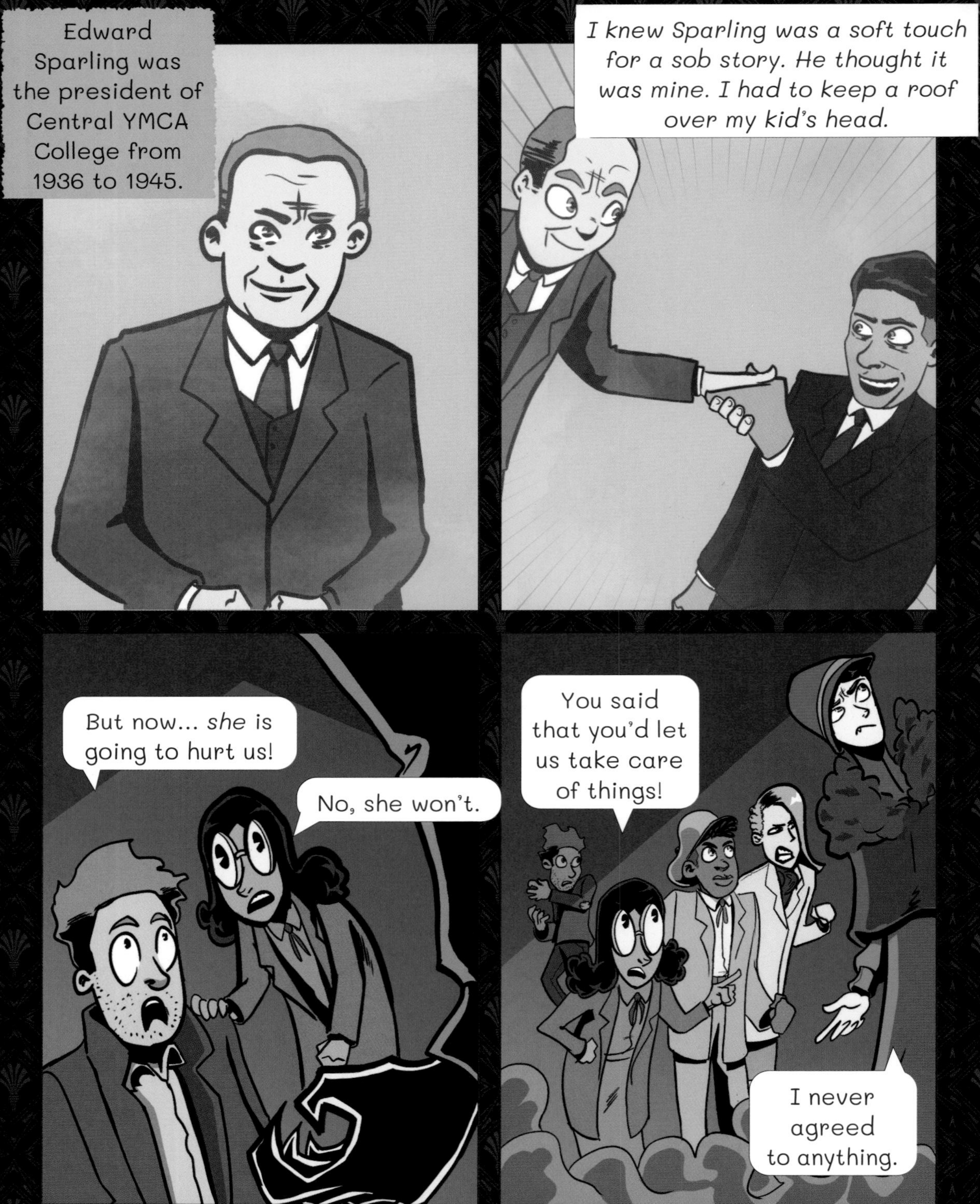
Edward Sparling was the president of Central YMCA College from 1936 to 1945.
I knew Sparling was a soft touch for a sob story. He thought it was mine. I had to keep a roof over my kid's head.
But now... *she* is going to hurt us!
No, she won't.
You said that you'd let us take care of things!
I never agreed to anything.

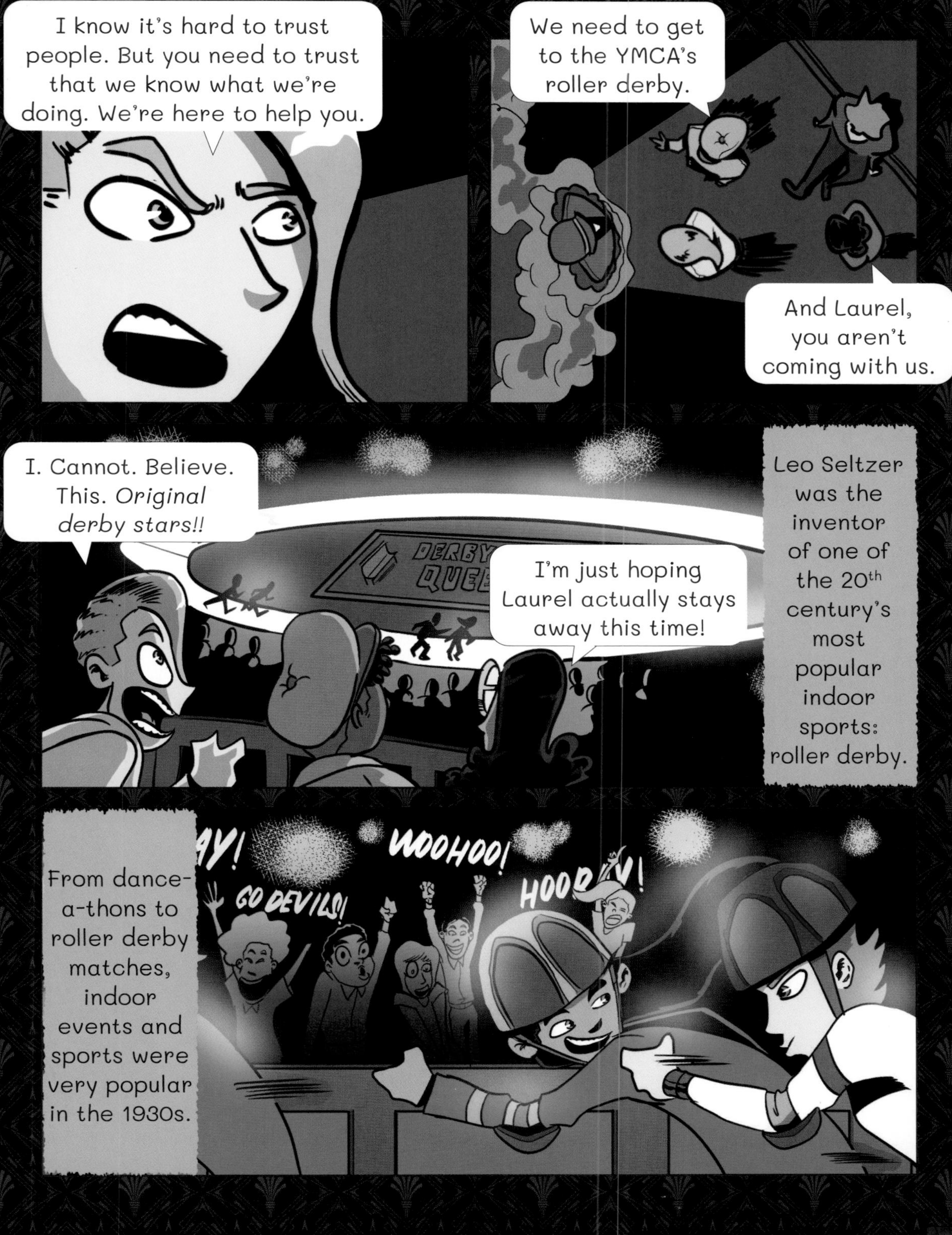

I know it's hard to trust people. But you need to trust that we know what we're doing. We're here to help you.
We need to get to the YMCA's roller derby.
And Laurel, you aren't coming with us.
I. Cannot. Believe. This. *Original derby stars!!*
I'm just hoping Laurel actually stays away this time!
Leo Seltzer was the inventor of one of the 20th century's most popular indoor sports: roller derby.
From dance-a-thons to roller derby matches, indoor events and sports were very popular in the 1930s.
WOOHOO!
GO DEVILS!

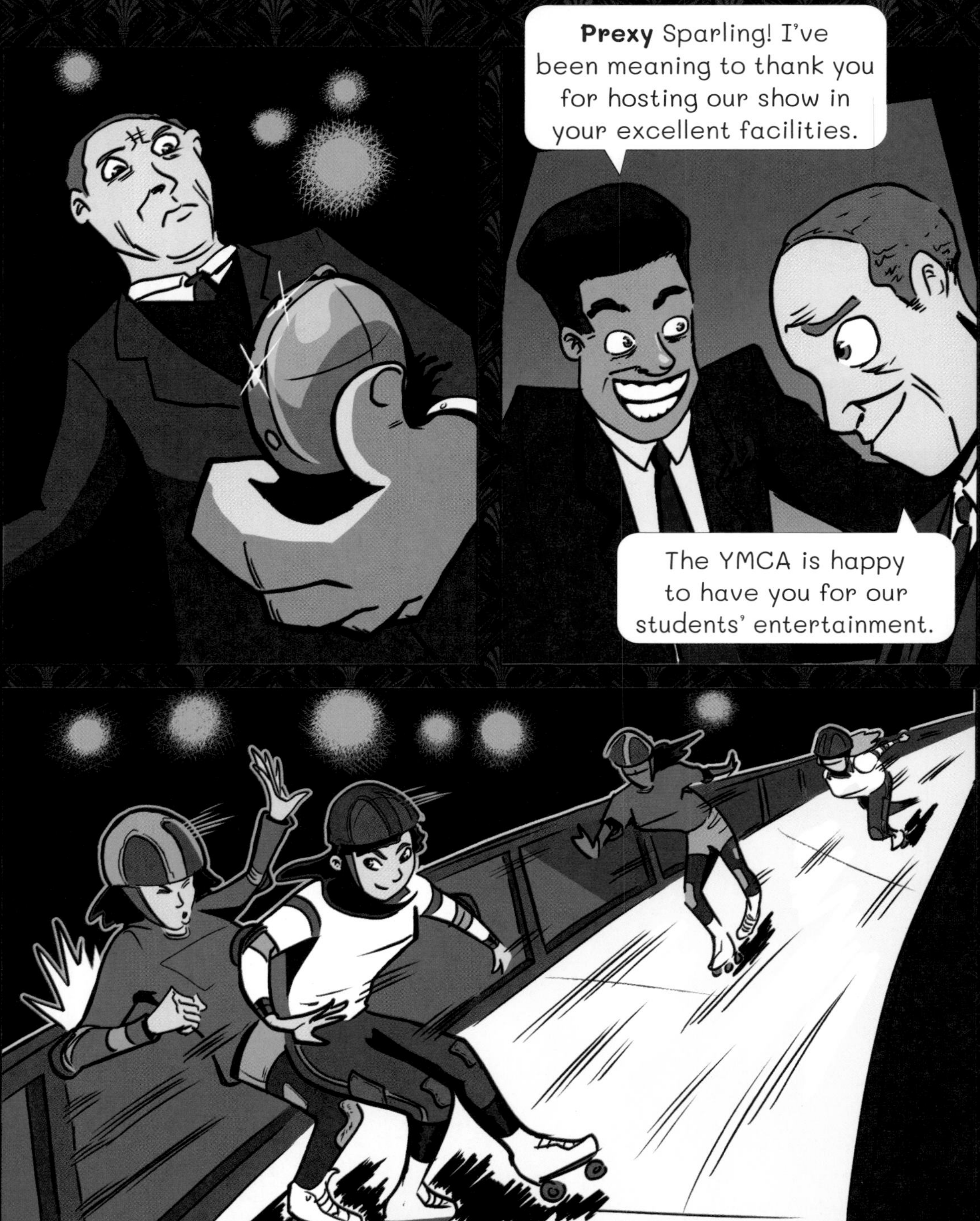
Prexy Sparling! I've been meaning to thank you for hosting our show in your excellent facilities.
The YMCA is happy to have you for our students' entertainment.

prexy: a common word for the president of a college or university

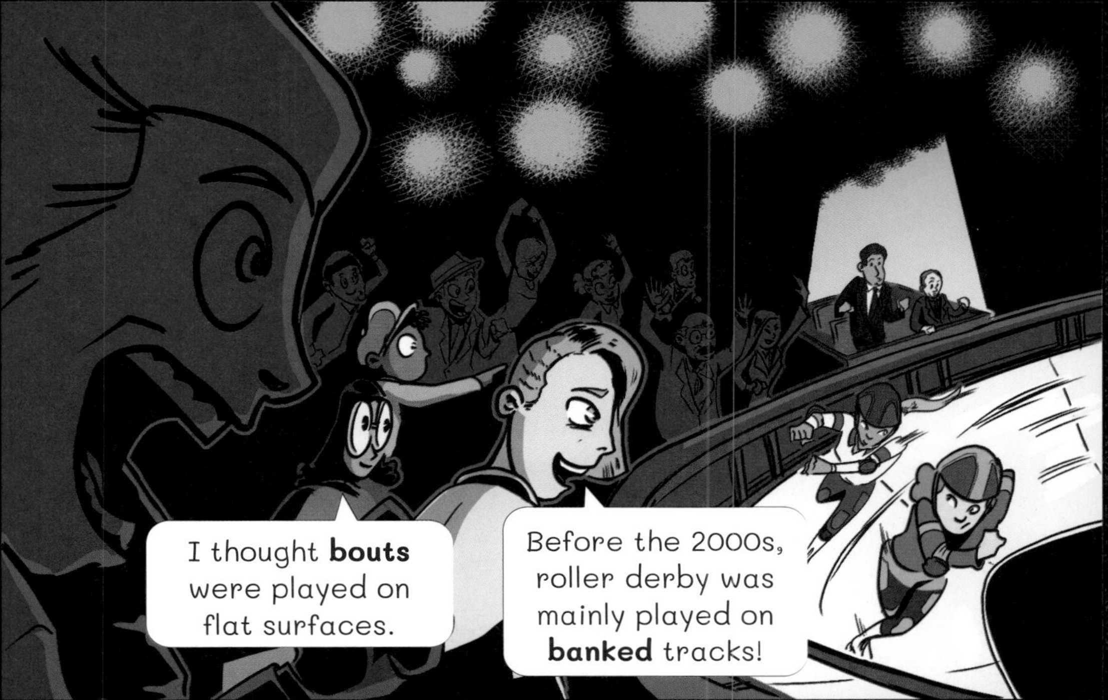
I thought **bouts** were played on flat surfaces.
Before the 2000s, roller derby was mainly played on **banked** tracks!

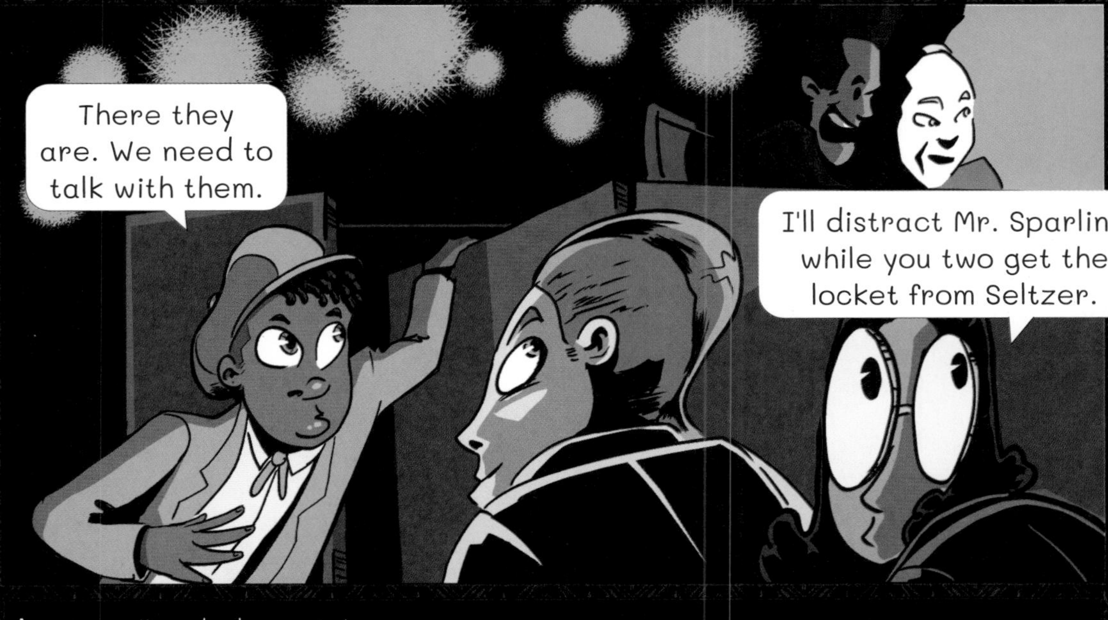
There they are. We need to talk with them.
I'll distract Mr. Sparling while you two get the locket from Seltzer.

bouts: roller derby matches

banked: raised and tilted sideways

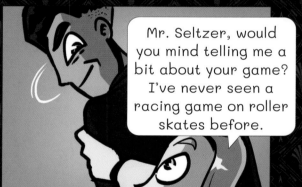

Mr. Seltzer, would you mind telling me a bit about your game? I've never seen a racing game on roller skates before.

Mr. Sparling, do you have a minute?

What can I do for you?

WHAT ARE VAMPIRES?

Vampires have been part of folk stories and folklore since the 1500s. Undead creatures like vampires are beings who have died and come back to life. But what is really known about vampires?

* Vampires must drink human blood to survive.

* They can transform into mist and animals.

* Vampires have supernatural speed and **agility**.

* They also have an incredible sense of smell.

While they have many powers, they also have weaknesses.

* Their skin cannot be in the sun. They often sleep all day and are out only at night.

It takes a vampire to create a vampire. Some people see vampires as reluctant heroes, who want to do good even though they may have dark natures.

agility: being able to move quickly and with ease

21

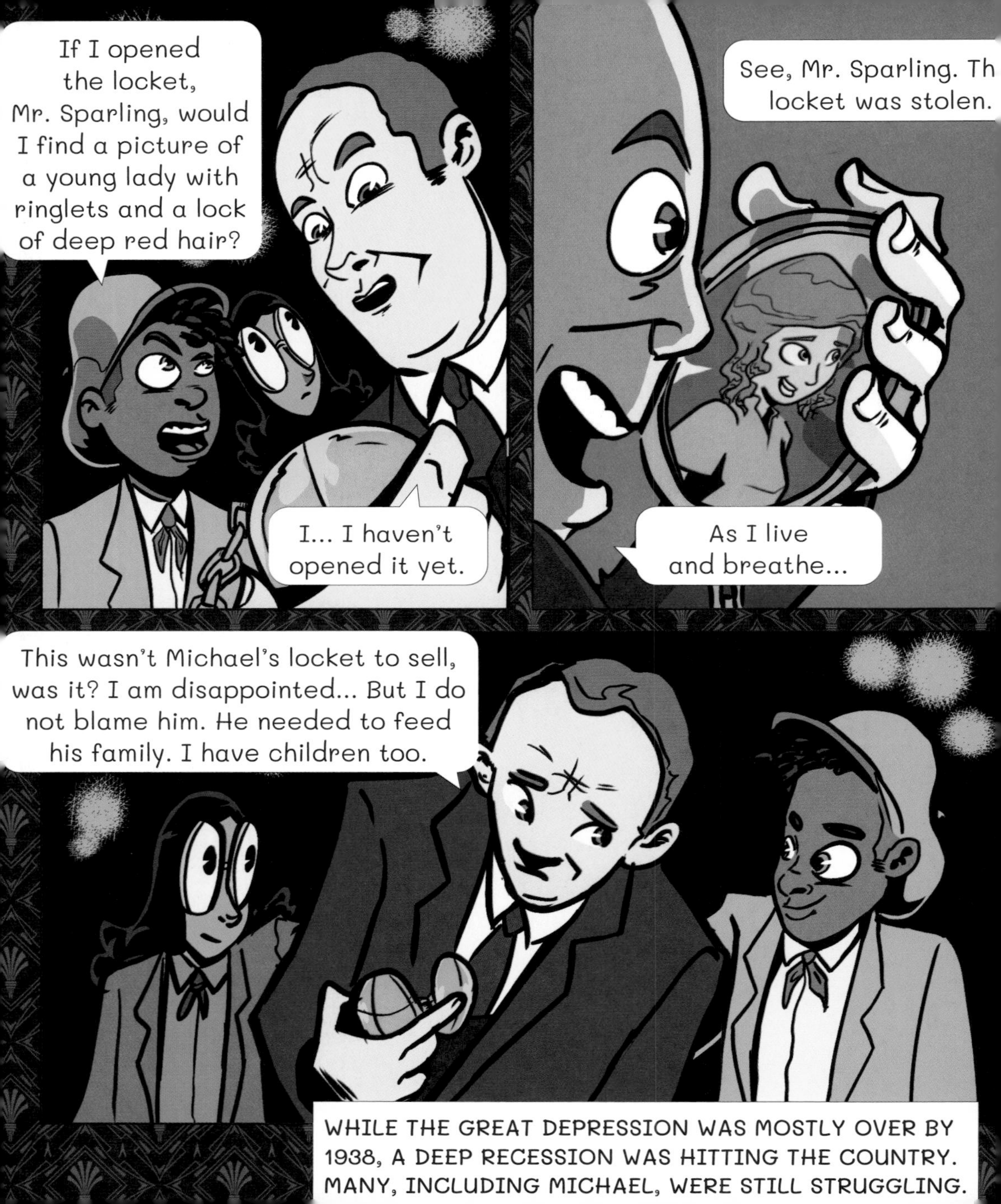
If I opened the locket, Mr. Sparling, would I find a picture of a young lady with ringlets and a lock of deep red hair?
I... I haven't opened it yet.
See, Mr. Sparling. Th locket was stolen.
As I live and breathe...
This wasn't Michael's locket to sell, was it? I am disappointed... But I do not blame him. He needed to feed his family. I have children too.
WHILE THE GREAT DEPRESSION WAS MOSTLY OVER BY 1938, A DEEP RECESSION WAS HITTING THE COUNTRY. MANY, INCLUDING MICHAEL, WERE STILL STRUGGLING.

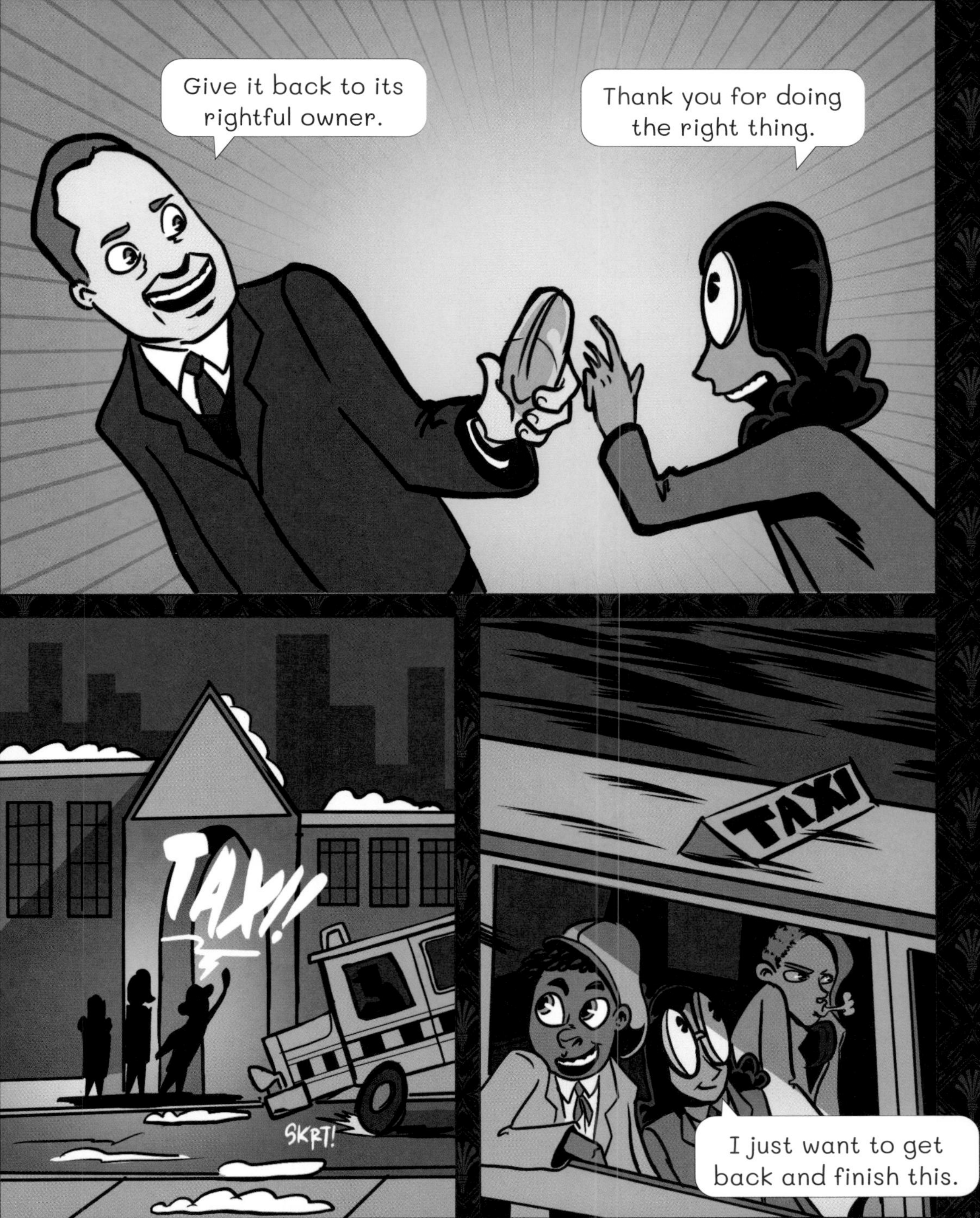
Give it back to its rightful owner.
Thank you for doing the right thing.
TAXI!!
SKRT!
TAXI
I just want to get back and finish this.

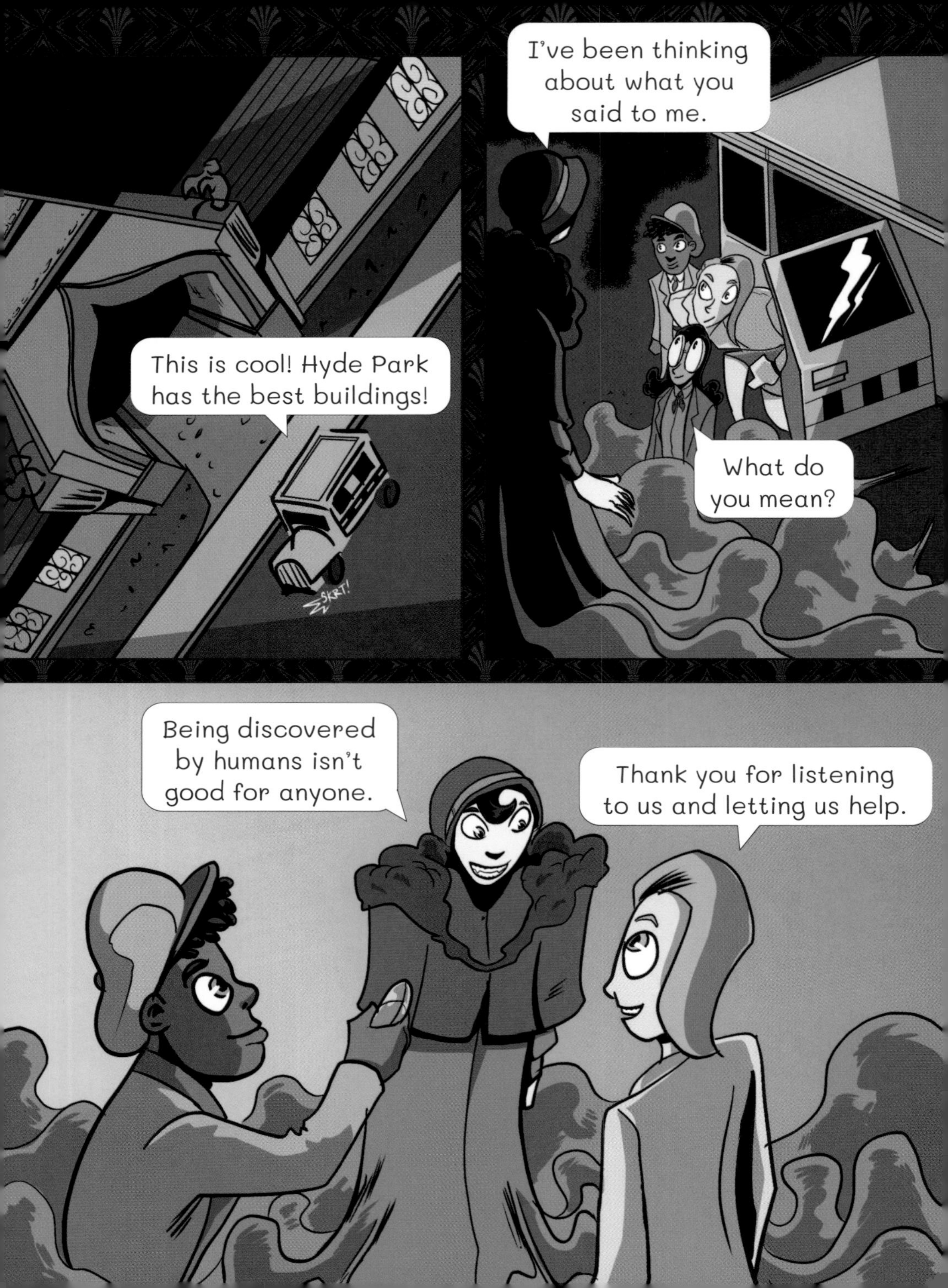
This is cool! Hyde Park has the best buildings!
SKRT!
I've been thinking about what you said to me.
What do you mean?
Being discovered by humans isn't good for anyone.
Thank you for listening to us and letting us help.

SURVIVAL TIPS

Surviving a vampire is difficult. They have superspeed and very sharp teeth. If they catch you, they will either kill you or turn you into a vampire. The best way to survive is to avoid them.

* Stay in the light and avoid shadows. Vampires can't be in the sun.
* If you must be outside at night, stay in crowded places.
* Never invite unknown people into your home. Vampires can only enter a home if they have been invited in.
* Vampires hate garlic. Having garlic will make a vampire not want to eat you.

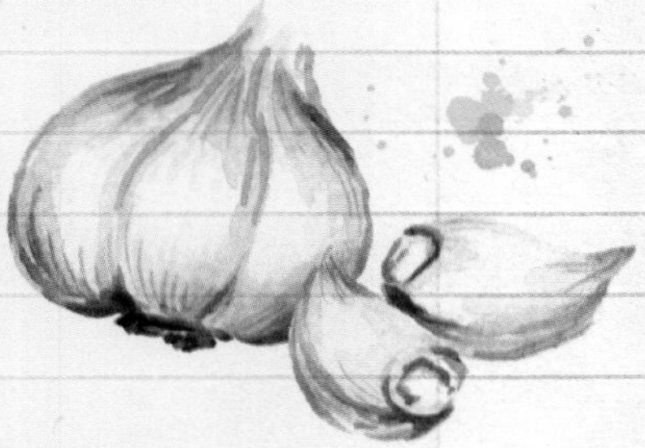

If you do get caught, be prepared.

* A vampire can be killed with a wooden stake through the heart.
* Silver weakens them and may give you a chance to escape.
* Religious symbols, like a cross, can hurt them.

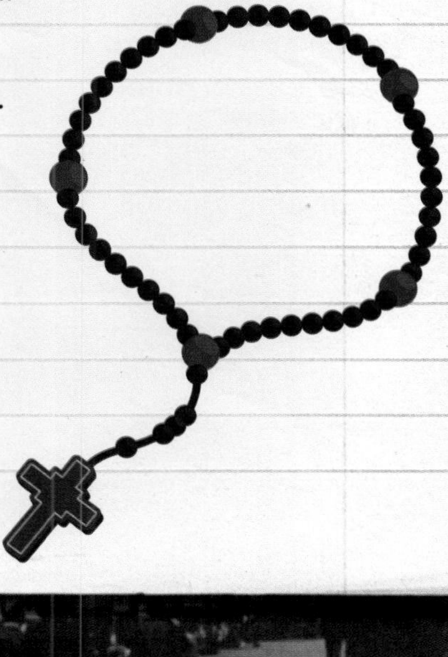

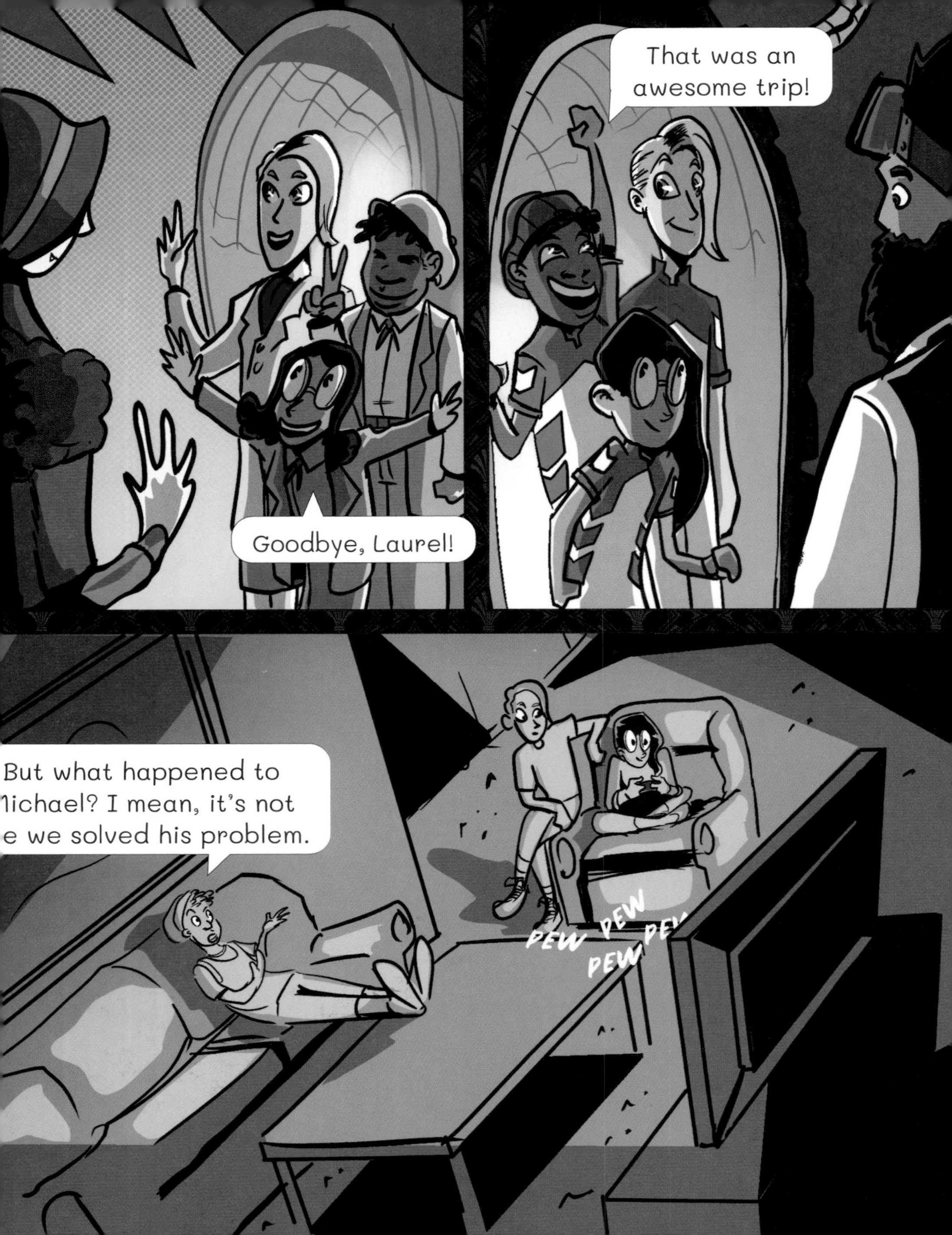
Goodbye, Laurel!
That was an awesome trip!
But what happened to ichael? I mean, it's not e we solved his problem.
PEW PEW PEW

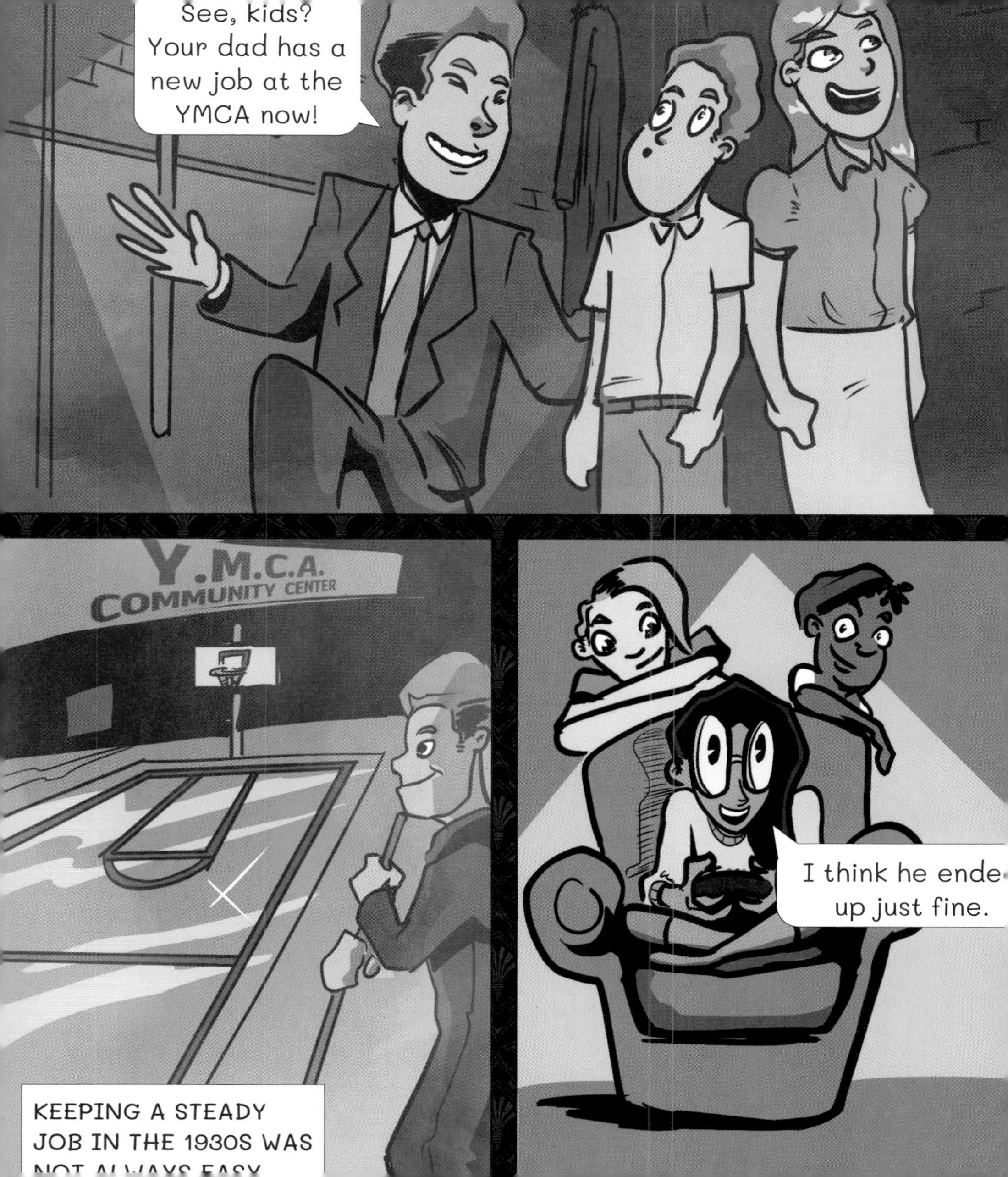
See, kids? Your dad has a new job at the YMCA now!
Y.M.C.A. COMMUNITY CENTER
KEEPING A STEADY JOB IN THE 1930S WAS
I think he ende up just fine.

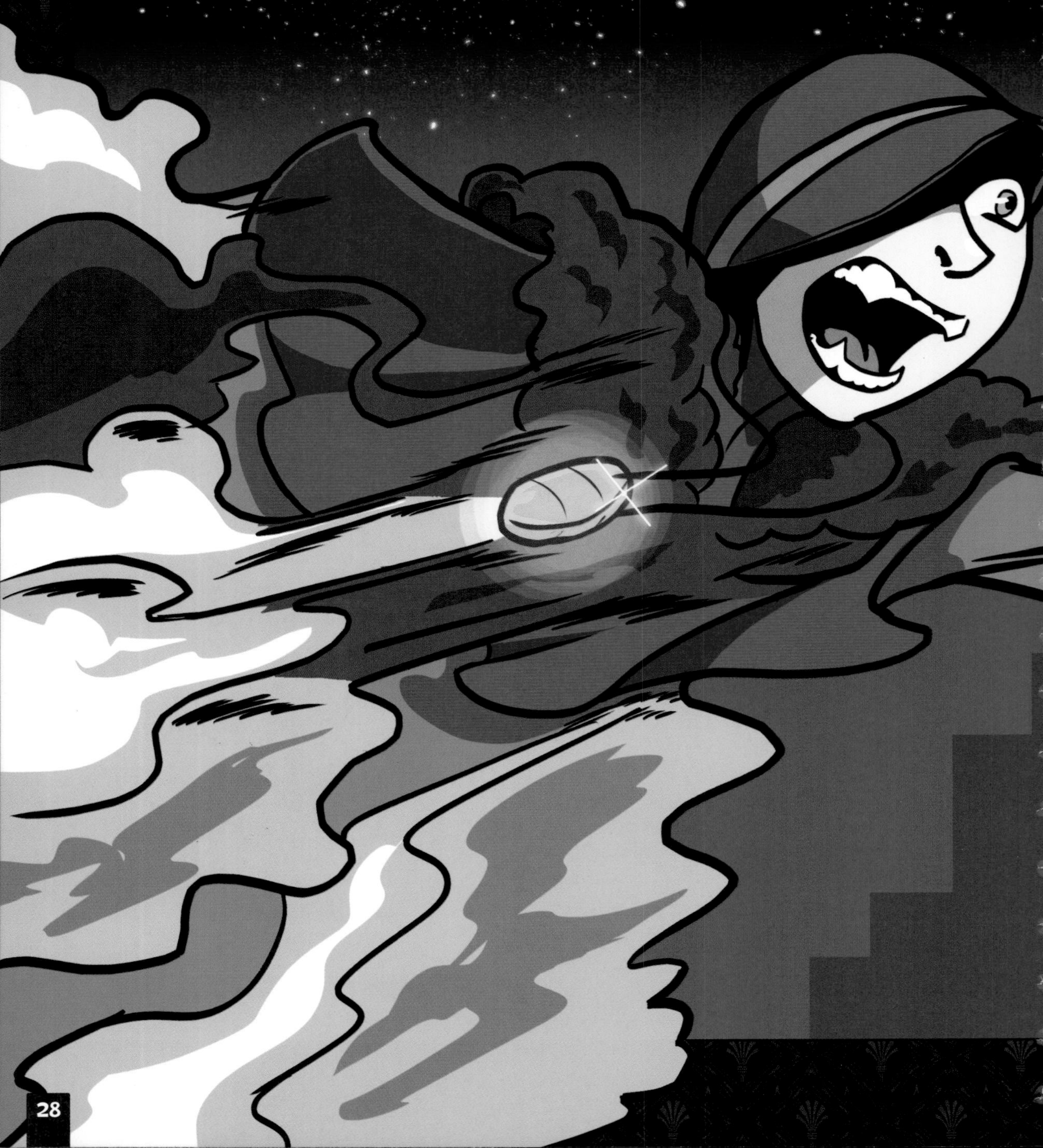

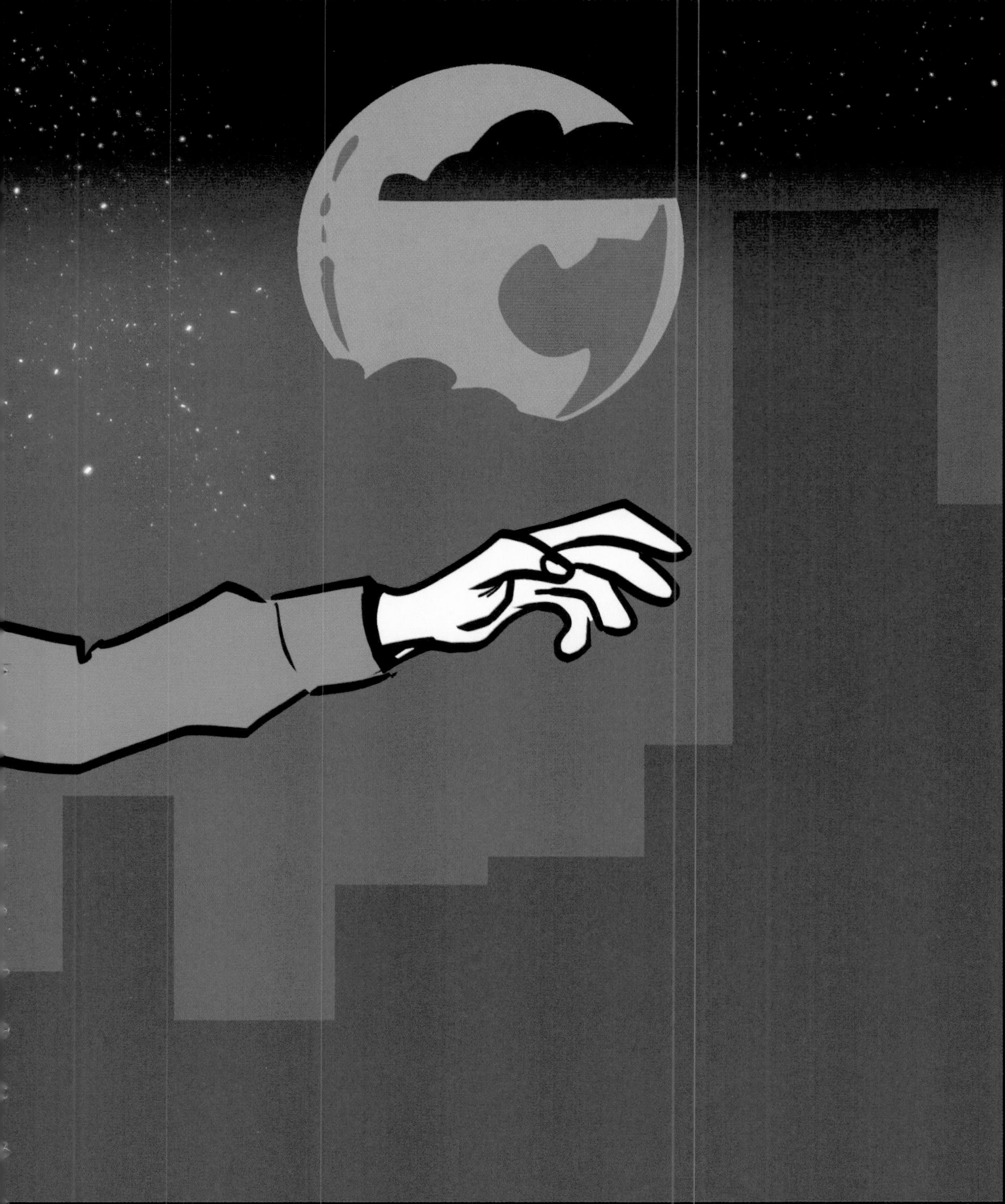

CREATE A SCRAPBOOK

Do you have an event in your life that is special? A family trip? A favorite holiday? Maybe you have a person in your life that means a lot, such as a favorite grandparent or a best friend. Making a scrapbook is a fun way to keep those memories close.

* Find a box or photo album that items can be stored in and kept safe.

* Collect **mementos**. These can be letters, cards, ticket stubs, or artwork that remind you of the time or person.

* Look through photos. Select your favorites to print.

Organize these items in order of how you experienced them. This way when you look back at this scrapbook, your memories are all in order. Now you can revisit your favorite people, places, and events any time!

mementos: objects kept to remember a person or event

LEARN MORE

BOOKS

Pascal, Janet B. *What Was the Great Depression?* New York, NY: Penguin Workshop, 2015.

Basil, Bobby. *Travel Bug Goes to Chicago: A Fun World Travel Guide for Kids.* Lexington, KY: Hazel Bazell, 2019.

WEBSITES

Ducksters—US History: The Great Depression
https://www.ducksters.com/history/us_1900s/great_depression.php

Choose Chicago—Chicago Facts
https://www.choosechicago.com/press-media/toolkit/chicago-facts

THE MONSTER HUNTER TEAM

JORGE
TÍO HECTOR'S NEPHEW, JORGE, LOVES MUSIC. AT 16 HE IS ONE OF THE OLDEST MONSTER HUNTERS AND THE LEADER OF THE GROUP.

FIONA
FIONA IS FIERCE AND PROTECTIVE. AT 16 SHE IS A ROLLER DERBY CHAMPION AND IS ONE OF JORGE'S CLOSEST FRIENDS.

AMY
AMY IS 15. SHE LOVES BOOKS AND HISTORY. AMY AND ELENA SPEND ALMOST EVERY WEEKEND TOGETHER. THEY ARE ATTACHED AT THE HIP.

MARCUS
MARCUS IS 14 AND IS WISE BEYOND HIS YEARS. HE IS A PROBLEM SOLVER, OFTEN GETTING THE GROUP OUT OF STICKY SITUATIONS.

ELENA
ELENA IS JORGE'S LITTLE SISTER AND TÍO HECTOR'S NIECE. AT 14, SHE IS THE HEART AND SOUL OF THE GROUP. ELENA IS KIND, THOUGHTFUL, AND SINCERE.

TÍO HECTOR
JORGE AND ELENA'S TIO IS THE MASTERMIND BEHIND THE MONSTER HUNTERS. HIS TIME TRAVEL MACHINE MAKES IT ALL POSSIBLE.

GLOSSARY

agility (uh-jil-ih-tee) being able to move quickly and with ease

bouts (BOUTS) roller derby matches

banked (BANGKT) raised and tilted sideways

Great Depression (GRAYT dih-PREH-shun) a great financial slump that began in 1929

locket (LAH-kit) a small case, usually made of gold or silver, that is worn on a necklace chain

mementos (muh-MEN-tohz) objects kept to remember a person or event

prexy (PREK-see) a common word for the president of a college or university

recession (ree-SEH-shun) a period of time when the trade and business is not doing well

tío (TEE-oh) "uncle" in Spanish

trainspotting (TRAYN-spah-ting) the hobby of going to railway stations and counting trains

INDEX